SACRAMENTO PUBLIC LIBRARY

Foundation

LEATHERBACK SEA TURTLE
MIGRATION

by Kelsey Jopp

Focus Readers is distributed by North Star Editions:
sales@northstareditions.com | 888-417-0195

Produced for Focus Readers by Red Line Editorial.

Content Consultant: Dr. Kate Mansfield, Marine Turtle Research Group, Department of Biology, University of Central Florida

Photographs ©: Brian J. Skerry/National Geographic Creative/Alamy, cover, 1, 18; David McFadden/AP Images, 4–5; IrinaK/Shutterstock Images, 7, 15, 21; Volina/Shutterstock Images, 9; Michael Patrick O'Neill/Science Source, 10–11; Stephanie Rousseau/Shutterstock Images, 12; Connie Merigo under NMFS Permit #15672, 16–17; ACEgan/Shutterstock Images, 23; Lynsey Allan/Shutterstock Images, 24–25; Richard Whitcombe/Shutterstock Images, 27; Al Woodson/US Fish and Wildlife Service, 28

ISBN
978-1-63517-909-5 (hardcover)
978-1-64185-011-7 (paperback)
978-1-64185-213-5 (ebook pdf)
978-1-64185-112-1 (hosted ebook)

Library of Congress Control Number: 2018932027

Printed in the United States of America
Mankato, MN
May, 2018

ABOUT THE AUTHOR

Kelsey Jopp is an editor, writer, and lifelong learner. She lives in Saint Paul, Minnesota, where she enjoys doing yoga and playing endless fetch with her sheltie, Teddy.

TABLE OF CONTENTS

CHAPTER 1

SLOW AND STEADY

When night falls, a female leatherback sea turtle swims to shore. She digs a deep hole in the sand and lays her eggs inside. She covers the eggs with sand. Then she returns to the water. She will swim thousands of miles back out to sea.

Two months later, the turtle is still swimming. But her eggs are hatching.

A female leatherback turtle prepares to leave a beach after burying her eggs.

The **hatchlings** are on their own as they crawl out of the hole. Right away, birds swoop down and grab a few of the hatchlings. The ones that remain crawl toward the open water. There, they will live and grow.

Scientists do not know exactly where the hatchlings go. They call this period "the lost years." After at least 10 years, the turtles will go to live near other adult turtles. The journey will be their first **migration**.

Leatherbacks travel across the ocean in search of food. They swim to feeding areas. These are spots of open water with a large supply of jellyfish to eat.

A leatherback hatchling crawls across the sand to reach the ocean.

Leatherbacks feed in cold waters. But every few years, they migrate back to warmer water to mate and lay eggs.

A female leatherback feeds on jellyfish for three to four years. She builds up her energy. Then she returns to mating areas and nesting grounds. Female leatherbacks make several nests on beaches. Then they swim back out to sea.

Male leatherbacks also migrate between feeding and mating areas. But unlike females, they do not go to nesting grounds. Male leatherbacks rarely go ashore.

Scientists divide leatherback sea turtles into seven types. Some types migrate more than others. The West Pacific leatherback migrates the most. These turtles nest on warm beaches in the western Pacific Ocean, such as those in Indonesia. When they are done nesting, they swim all the way to the West Coast of the United States. They cover more than 6,000 miles (9,600 km) of ocean in 10 to 12 months.

Most adult leatherbacks return to the same feeding areas again and again. This means the turtles follow specific paths. But their migration method is a mystery scientists have not yet solved.

PATHS IN THE PACIFIC

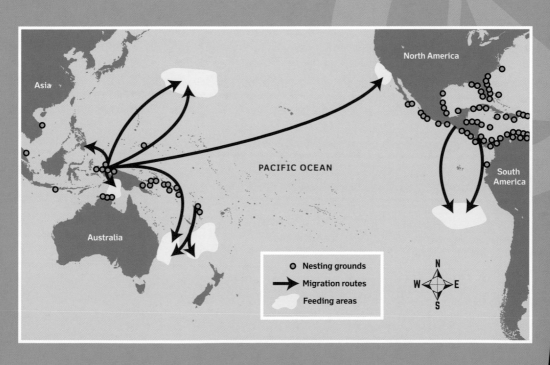

Asia

North America

PACIFIC OCEAN

South America

Australia

○ Nesting grounds
➤ Migration routes
Feeding areas

N
W ◆ E
S

CHAPTER 2

NAVIGATING THE WATERS

The leatherback sea turtle's body has adapted to help it survive the long journey. Leatherbacks are the world's largest sea turtle. Some are as long as 6.5 feet (2.0 m). The leatherback's large size helps the turtle swim against strong waves. Its size also keeps the turtle warm in deep, cold water.

Leatherback sea turtles migrate farther than any other sea turtle.

Leatherbacks dive deeper than any other reptile. Some leatherbacks swim as deep as 4,100 feet (1,250 m). The leatherback's shell protects the turtle in deep water. Most sea turtles have a hard shell. But a leatherback's shell is

MADE FOR MIGRATION

Pink skin patch
(possibly used to
detect the sun)

Flexible shell
with bony plates

Powerful front
flippers

660 to 1,100 pounds
(300 to 500 kg)

4 to 6 feet long
(1.2 to 1.8 m)

flexible. It feels similar to leather. As the turtle swims deeper, the force of the water becomes stronger. The turtle's shell bends under the water's pressure. This keeps the water from breaking the turtle's bones.

Scientists have ideas about why leatherbacks dive so deep. Swimming in deep water may protect the turtles from predators that live in shallow waters. Diving might also help the leatherbacks **navigate**. Some scientists think the turtles notice changes in chemicals at different ocean levels. These chemicals might serve as important clues. They might guide the turtles toward food.

Scientists think leatherbacks may have a sense that works similar to a compass. Animals with this ability use clues from Earth's **magnetic field**. They sense the angle at which the field hits Earth. This helps the animals know where they are.

BABY TALK

Scientists studied a nest of leatherback eggs. They found that the turtles inside the eggs made noises. Most noises were chirps and grunts. But one was more complex. This sound had two tones. When the first egg hatched, the complex sound stopped. Scientists think the turtles use this sound to plan hatching times. If eggs hatch at the same time, the turtles can travel together. This gives them a better chance of surviving their race to the ocean.

Baby turtles must crawl up to the surface after hatching.

Leatherbacks may also use clues from the sun. A leatherback has a thin patch of pink skin on its head. Scientists think the turtle can detect the sun through the patch. In this way, the turtle tells time. The turtle senses when days are shorter. It knows the seasons are changing and that it is time to migrate.

CHAPTER 3

TURTLE TRACKING

Leatherback turtles spend most of their lives at sea. This makes it difficult to study the animal. Scientists cannot follow leatherbacks into deep, open water. Fortunately, scientists can use satellite tags. These devices help track the turtles' movements. Scientists attach satellite tags to a turtle's back.

A satellite tag goes on a turtle's shell and shows scientists its location.

 Scientists catch and release leatherbacks to put tags on them.

As the turtle swims, the tag sends signals to satellites orbiting Earth. The satellites pass the signals to a computer. This shows scientists the turtle's location. They can tell when and where the turtle moves.

One team of scientists put satellite tags on 46 female leatherbacks. They tracked the turtles for three years. Each year, the turtles took the same route. But the ocean's **current** often pushed them from their path. Scientists made some calculations. Without the effect of the currents, the turtles were swimming on a narrow path. They were headed straight for the South Pacific Gyre.

The South Pacific Gyre is a large, empty area in the Pacific Ocean. Scientists did not know why the turtles would go there. There could be prey far below the surface. But the water is too deep for scientists to find out.

Still, scientists hope to use the information to help leatherbacks. They can direct fishing boats away from the turtles' migration path. This would prevent turtles from being caught.

Satellite tagging helps scientists learn more about leatherbacks. But it can also

ODD TURTLE OUT

One of the 46 turtles in the study took a different route. This turtle swam along the coast of Central America. It stayed near the coast for at least 588 days. That's when the turtle's tag stopped working. Scientists aren't sure why the turtle took a different route. In the past, a whole group of turtles might have followed this route. But the others might have died from dangers along the coast.

Leatherbacks face many dangers as they swim to and from the shore.

be harmful. Some tags can increase a turtle's **drag**. This makes it harder for the turtles to swim. As a result, the turtles may swim more slowly. This change of pace affects their migration. It can also make it harder for them to catch prey.

AN EPIC JOURNEY

In 2003, a leatherback turtle left the warm waters of Indonesia. It had a satellite tag attached to its back. Scientists used the tag to track the turtle. The leatherback traveled a distance of 12,774 miles (20,558 km). It was the longest recorded migration of any sea **vertebrate**.

The leatherback swam across the Pacific Ocean for 647 days. Swordfish and tuna likely crossed its path. The turtle might have also passed other leatherbacks. These turtles had been feeding along the West Coast of the United States. Now, they were returning to warmer waters.

At one point, the turtle crossed the **equator**. Here, it faced strong, quick currents. Afterward, it passed close to one of Hawaii's islands. Finally, the turtle reached the coast of Oregon. This area has many jellyfish. The turtle would eat and rest

Sometimes fish cling to a leatherback turtle during its long journey.

there. After a few years, it would make the long return journey.

CHAPTER 4

SAVING THE LEATHERBACKS

All around the world, leatherback populations are decreasing. The Pacific leatherback is the world's most **endangered** sea turtle. Since the 1980s, its population has dropped by more than 95 percent. Humans are the biggest threat to leatherbacks. Some people take the turtles' eggs before they hatch.

People who collect and sell leatherback eggs are damaging leatherback populations.

Then they sell the eggs. This practice is called poaching. In many countries, poaching is against the law. Even so, people still do it.

Fishing is also a threat to leatherbacks. Turtles can become tangled in fishing line. When this happens, they cannot get back up to the surface to breathe. Thousands of turtles drown in fishing line every year.

Sometimes, fishing boats accidentally catch leatherbacks instead of fish. To save their fishing hooks, people cut off the turtle's flipper. Then they return the turtle to the sea. Without its front flipper, the leatherback may not survive.

A plastic bag can be fatal to a leatherback turtle.

Pollution is another threat to leatherbacks. When humans litter, trash can end up in the ocean. Leatherbacks mistake plastic bags for jellyfish. They eat the bags. But the plastic blocks their digestive system. This can cause the turtles to starve to death.

Leatherback turtles often return to the beaches where they were born to make nests.

Many scientists are working to protect leatherbacks. The Leatherback Trust (TLT) is a **conservation** program. It works with countries to create protection areas. Most of these areas are leatherback nesting beaches. But TLT hopes to expand the areas to migration paths.

In Indonesia, conservationists search the beaches for leatherback nests. When they find a nest, they protect it. However, leatherbacks spend years migrating. That means beach conservation is not enough. Humans must learn how to protect the turtles at sea. Until that happens, these amazing animals will be in danger.

THE GREAT TURTLE RACE

In 2007, a scientist held the Great Turtle Race. Before the race, the scientist tracked 11 migrating leatherbacks. Their migration took six months. Afterward, the scientist sped up the tracking data. Over the course of two weeks, people could watch the sped-up migration online. They placed votes for which turtle they thought would finish first. The Great Turtle Race helped more people learn about leatherbacks and the threats to their survival.

LEATHERBACK SEA TURTLE MIGRATION

Write your answers on a separate piece of paper.

1. Write a sentence summarizing one threat that leatherbacks face while migrating.

2. Which part of a leatherback's body do you think is most useful for migrating? Why?

3. How do scientists track leatherbacks?
   - **A.** fishing
   - **B.** nesting
   - **C.** tagging

4. What would happen if a leatherback sea turtle did not leave its feeding area?
   - **A.** It would die of hunger.
   - **B.** It would not be able to lay eggs.
   - **C.** It would be caught by fishing boats.

Answer key on page 32.

GLOSSARY

conservation
The careful protection of plants, animals, and natural resources so they are not lost or wasted.

current
A water movement that goes in a certain direction.

drag
The force of water pushing back against a moving object.

endangered
In danger of dying out.

equator
An imaginary line that runs around the middle of Earth.

hatchlings
Young animals that are born from eggs.

magnetic field
The space around an object (such as a moon or planet) in which its magnetic force can be detected.

migration
When animals move to a different location.

navigate
To find one's way while traveling.

vertebrate
An animal that has a backbone and a skeleton.

TO LEARN MORE

BOOKS

Grunbaum, Mara. *Sea Turtles*. New York: Children's Press, 2018.

Hirsch, Rebecca E. *Thousand-Mile Fliers and Other Amazing Migrators*. Minneapolis: Lerner Publications, 2017.

Swinburne, Stephen R. *Sea Turtle Scientist*. Boston: Houghton Mifflin Harcourt, 2014.

NOTE TO EDUCATORS

Visit **www.focusreaders.com** to find lesson plans, activities, links, and other resources related to this title.

INDEX

Answer Key: 1. Answers will vary; **2.** Answers will vary; **3.** C; **4.** B